A

CRITICAL COMMENTARY

ON

Milton's 'Samson Agonistes'

ALAN RUDRUM

MACMILLAN
London · Melbourne · Toronto
ST MARTIN'S PRESS
New York

MISSOURI BAPTIST COLLEGE LIBRARY

© Alan Rudrum 1969

First published 1969 by
MACMILLAN AND CO LTD
Little Essex Street London WC2
and also at Bombay Calcutta and Madras
Macmillan South Africa (Publishers) Pty Ltd Johannesburg
The Macmillan Company of Australia Pty Ltd Melbourne
The Macmillan Company of Canada Ltd Toronto
St Martin's Press Inc New York
Gill and Macmillan Ltd Dublin

Printed in Great Britain by
ROBERT MACLEHOSE AND CO LTD
The University Press Glasgow

73-1051

This book, my last on Milton in this series, is dedicated, with much love, to Heather Rudrum and our three children, Helga, Nicolas and Ursula

Contents

Foreword	6
Acknowledgements	6
Abbreviations	6
A Note on Quotations	7
Introduction	9
The Difficulties	10
The Subject	13
A Note on the Title	17
Samson and Greek Tragedy	
'Concentration' and Milton's Language	21
Samson (1–114)	22
Samson and the Chorus (115–330)	25
Samson and Manoah (326–651)	33
Chorus (652–709)	38
Samson and Dalila (710–1009)	42
Chorus (1010–60)	48
Harapha (1061–1267)	50
Samson and the Chorus (1268–96)	56
Samson and the Officer (1297–1426)	58
The Chorus (1427–40)	60
Manoah, Chorus, and Messenger (1441–1659)	61
Questions for Discussion	68
Further Reading	69

Foreword

The present series of Critical Commentaries is offered in the belief that, faced with a work of exceptional density of texture or complication of structure, the reader may be helped in his appreciation by a 'conducted tour' or point-by-point critical exposition. These commentaries are intended as a supplement to the material normally supplied in a scholarly edition and not, of course, as a substitute for it. A 'further-reading list' will normally be provided, together with selected questions for discussion.

Acknowledgements

I am grateful to the University of Adelaide for granting me a year's study-leave, during which I began work on this book; to the ever-helpful staff of the British Museum Reading Room, where I did most of my preparatory reading; and to my former students in The Queen's University of Belfast for their kindly reception of my lectures on Milton.

Abbreviations

OED   *The Oxford English Dictionary*
PL   *Paradise Lost*
SM   *The Student's Milton*, ed. F. A. Patterson

A Note on Quotations

I have quoted throughout from Helen Darbishire's edition of 1955; since many of my readers will be using other editions, I have given line-references for all quotations. Anyone who is in difficulties with my quotations can quickly look them up in a modernised edition.

A. R.

Introduction

Samson Agonistes has never been the most popular of Milton's works, though many readers have felt it to be one of the most powerful. In recent years hostile critics have directed a double attack: on its dramatic deficiencies, and on its language. There is no real novelty in this. Johnson said that 'it is only by a blind confidence in the reputation of Milton that a drama can be praised in which the intermediate parts have neither cause nor consequence, neither hasten nor retard the catastrophe'. Of Milton's language Johnson complained that 'through all his greater works there prevails an uniform peculiarity of *diction*, a mode and cast of expression which . . . is so far removed from common use that an unlearned reader . . . finds himself surprised by a new language'. Johnson's criticisms are comprehensive. It is not surprising if modern dislikers of *Samson* have done little more than elaborate on them. Of course hostility is not the whole story; but it is notable that few of the professional readers who experience *Samson* as a powerful drama have felt able to explain and justify this response simply by reference to the work itself. They have thought it necessary to explore the various 'traditions' behind the work, in order to discover relevant attitudes and critical terminologies. There is much that is admirable about this scholarly work; but one cannot help but be suspicious about some of its results – for of course in each case the 'key' to the *Samson* enigma turns out to be the tradition on which the particular scholar has been working. So we are told in turn that *Samson* is primarily Hebraic in inspiration, and that we shall best understand it in the light of various books of the Old Testament; that it is primarily Christian in feeling and idea, and is best illuminated by the various interpretations of the Samson legend developed in the Christian centuries; that of course it is Greek in construction, feeling and idea, and we shall best approach it via Aeschylus, Sophocles and Euripides. None of these suggestions, surely, can be exclusively true, and we shall be wise to accept gratefully the factual information their exponents present, and be chary of accepting any exclusivist critical theory. If, for example, we are told that 'beyond cavil . . . we may call the fact of Samson's death a "debt" to Sophocles' (W. R. Parker, *Milton's Debt to Greek Tragedy*, 152), we shall do well to enquire whether the debt to Judges xvi 30 was not even greater. A little knowledge of Milton, and a little common sense, will surely lead us to expect a fusion in *Samson* of Hebrew, Greek and Christian elements, such as we frequently find elsewhere in his work. The task of criticism is not so much to disentangle the various traditions informing the work as to explore the final product. *Samson* can be appreciated (and, if not fully understood, at least not radically misunderstood) by readers knowing little of the scholarly 'background'. People coming to it for the first time frequently find it difficult, but they find it rewarding; and the difficulties are probably best overcome by reading and re-reading *Samson* rather than by plunging into 'scholarship'.

THE DIFFICULTIES

On the face of it, *Samson* should not be very difficult. The story is familiar: it must be one of those Old Testament stories of which almost everyone, even nowadays, has at least a vague knowledge. So far as ideas go, it is surely easier than the 'Nativity Ode'; it does not contain a daunting number of classical and mythological allusions; and its language is probably no more difficult than in other works of Milton.

What sort of difficulties do we then encounter in *Samson*? In trying to answer this question it is worth while to distinguish two kinds of difficulty. First, a poem may be difficult to read with understanding and enjoyment; second, a poem may be difficult to discuss; it may seem not to offer footholds to criticism.

Now some of the reasons why, on the face of it, *Samson* should not be very difficult to read, could also be advanced as reasons why it is difficult to discuss. Critics thrive on obvious difficulties; it is always a help to a teacher if a poem or play contains ideas, allusions, words that are likely to be unfamiliar to his audience. That *Samson* has so far received relatively little purely critical attention may be due to the fact that it is not rich in obvious difficulties.

To return to the more important kind of difficulty; is *Samson* difficult to read and, if so, why? There is, first, a difficulty which arises from its *form*. The first serious drama most of us read is likely to be Shakespeare rather than Greek tragedy. There is nothing really difficult about the structure of *Samson*, but unfamiliarity puts up a sort of smoke-screen, a tenuous but opaque barrier. This, then, amounts to a 'psychological' problem: strangeness rather than intrinsic difficulty causes the trouble.

There is another 'psychological' difficulty of a more fundamental kind. This has to do with the 'mood' or 'spirit' of the work. *Samson*'s intensity, its almost entire aloofness from humour or romanticism, its stark concentration on the figure of the hero, combine to make its appreciation, for modern man, a feat of emotional and intellectual athleticism. Figuratively speaking, prayer and fasting are needed. In this respect, the only modern dramatist I can think of whose work has any resemblance to Milton's is Samuel Beckett; the demands made upon the audience by such a play as *End Game* are similar to those made by *Samson*; and one doubts if there has ever been a performance of a Beckett play from which some members of the audience did not flee before the end. Yet, if concentration and intensity of this order seem alien to our modern temperament, something in our nature longs for it. We dimly apprehend the truth of Aristotle's purgation-theory, restated by Milton in the Preface to *Samson*. In the total concentration on the tragic experience which this poem demands there is something medicinal to human nature.

There are two terms here, which may be separated for discussion though their significance derives from their fusion. *Concentration*: one of the mottoes of our age might be T. S. Eliot's 'distracted from distraction by distraction'. Most people find something fortifying in the mere *act* of concentration, whether upon a game of chess, a mathematical problem, or a piece of music. *The tragic experience*: one of the elements in our experience of tragedy is our sympathetic identification with the tragic hero. In reading the play properly, we *are* Samson – and at the same time we are not. Our contemplation of his sufferings and his moral struggles blends the detachment and objectivity which we might bring to the affairs of a complete stranger, with the understanding and inwardness of sympathy that we might bring to – ourselves. One 'technique' of ordering our spiritual lives involves learning to look upon our past deeds and motives as objectively as if they belonged to a complete stranger. In this way the mistakes, humiliations, sins of our own past are to be transmuted into the possibility of future righteousness. Probably few people undertake such spiritual exercises; perhaps few are really capable of doing so. I mention them here because I think that there is a genuine parallel in the proper experience of tragedy; and that it is through this blend of sympathy and detachment that 'catharsis' comes about. That it really does come about is something that only one's own individual experience can entitle one to have an opinion on.

THE SUBJECT

The story of Samson is probably one of the more familiar Old Testament stories, even today. However, many of us know it only in vague memories of Sunday school, and it is worth while turning to Judges xiii–xvi and reading it for ourselves. It is then soon apparent that the story *has* to be modified, not simply in the interests of children at Sunday school but to make it suitable as a Christian story for an audience of any age: Samson's sexual adventurism and barbaric violence fit awkwardly into any regular pattern of a Christian hero.

In fact, the history of the Samson legend, from earliest times, is one of modification and interpretation. When Milton came to consider its suitability for drama it had more than two thousand years of interpretation around it. Our view of Milton's drama must be based upon a reading of *Samson* itself; but the history of the interpretation of the legend helps us to understand how it was that Milton could discern a tragic hero in the Old Testament roughneck.

The oral tradition behind the first written version of the legend is probably as old as twelve centuries B.C. It was probably written down in the tenth century B.C., and the first important modification came about in a drastic revision done about three hundred years later. The revision stressed monotheism (the true God versus Dagon), divine justice (the Israelites punished for their sins), and divine mercy (God sending Samson as a champion to deliver Israel out of the hands of the Philistines). In the revision a number of minor interpolations were made in chapters xiv–xvi; while chapter xiii represents, almost entirely, additional material. It is interesting to read the story in Judges twice, on the second reading omitting chapter xiii. It then becomes obvious how far the revision goes in giving the story a theological interpretation. Samson's birth becomes an event specially ordained by God, marked by the appearance of an angel. He becomes, not just an exceptionally strong man, but a man whose strength is supernatural, God-given, granted in order that the divine purpose for Israel, the Chosen People of God, should be advanced. This thirteenth chapter transforms Samson from a national folk-hero into a special agent of God.

The history of the interpretation of the Samson legend in the Christian centuries is so rich and complex that I can only refer to a few important points. St Paul, in exhorting the Hebrews to be steadfast in the faith, called a long roll of their own national heroes who had been victorious by faith. Among these is Samson (Hebrews xi 32). Later Christian writers accepted these Old Testament figures, who had been specially called and favoured by God, as saints, so that when, in *Samson* (1288), the Chorus refers to 'Saints', the anachronism is one hallowed by Christian usage. During the first seven centuries after Christ interpretation was of three kinds, making of Samson in turn a Christian saint, an allegorical figure of Christ, and the equivalent of Hercules. This third interpretation was recalled by Milton when he illustrated the shame of Adam and Eve after the Fall:

> So rose the *Danite* strong
> *Herculean Samson* from the Harlot-lap
> Of *Philistean Dalilah*, and wak'd
> Shorn of his strength, They destitute and bare
> Of all thir vertue. (*PL* IX 1059 ff.)

Of course, Christian commentators were quite aware of the

Introduction

difficulties involved in turning the brawling Israelite into a Christian hero. They achieved the transmutation partly by finding acceptable allegorical interpretations of some of the coarser events in the Judges story (St Augustine interpreted Samson's visit to the harlot as prefiguring Christ lying in the bonds of death!); partly by concluding that in the case of the elect, God may waive moral rules. The commandment against suicide did not apply in Samson's case because he was impelled by God, and his self-destruction was inseparable from the destruction of the idolators (see *Samson* 1664 ff.). It is striking that these feats of interpretation all run in the same direction: 'Samson was a saint, *therefore* certain apparent incongruities have to be explained in line with that fact', not 'There are too many difficulties, therefore Samson could not have been a saint'. The sanctity of Samson seems to have been quite firmly established.

During the scholastic period (roughly A.D. 1000–1500) there was a development in interpretation which foreshadows Milton's treatment. Less attention was paid to Samson's sensational feats, and more to the psychology of the Dalila episode. The scholastics gave much more attention than previous interpreters to the last period of Samson's life – his betrayal and capture, his blindness, his labour at the mill, and his death. The last phase of Samson's career was on at least one occasion compared with the last days of Christ, in a Palm Sunday sermon.

The comparison of Samson with Christ was widely accepted from the scholastic period until Milton's own time. Thomas Hayne's *General View of the Holy Scriptures*, published in 1640, tabulates nine allegorical parallels. For example, the births of both Samson and Christ were foretold by angels; both had enemies who sought to do them mischief; both obtained their victories by the spirit of God, without men's aid; Samson was betrayed by the kiss of Dalila, Christ by that of Judas – and so on. We should remember that the allegorical tradition, in which Samson was treated as a figure of Christ, was still very much alive in the seventeenth century, and that Milton must have been aware of it. How far, if at all, does his treatment in *Samson Agonistes* fall within this particular tradition of interpretation? *Samson* has been called primarily Greek. It has been called primarily Hebrew. Is it perhaps primarily Christian?

This has necessarily been a very brief treatment of the Samson 'tradition', but it should be clear that in deciding to write a tragedy about Samson, Milton had a great deal to contemplate besides the Book of Judges. We may eventually decide that *Samson Agonistes* is a profoundly original work, but if so it is original *within* a constant stream of thought and discussion of Samson as a Christian hero.

Milton was not the first to notice the suitability of Samson for a tragic hero. He was the hero of many plays, in Latin and the modern European languages, written during the sixteenth century. Salianus (1620) had discussed the last days of Samson in terms of the theory of tragedy given by Aristotle in the *Poetics*. In other respects the current of thought in the seventeenth century was flowing towards *Samson Agonistes*: stress was increasingly laid on Samson as one whose tragedy came about through a failure to live up to the call from God; and emphasis on his physical suffering was giving way to interest in the spiritual and psychological aspects of his ruin. Any tragedy arising out of these tendencies of thought would necessarily stress Samson's inner life rather than the events of his career.

When we read Judges xiii–xvi, and when we consider the Samson 'tradition', two things become clear: first, *Samson Agonistes* is very far from being a rehash of the mere Bible story – the element of *interpretation* in Milton's treatment is very strong. Second, certain important features of *Samson Agonistes* are in line with traditional Christian views, particularly as these developed towards Milton's own lifetime. To recognise that *Samson* was not produced in a vacuum is not to deny its originality; it is still profoundly original both in idea and in execution.

A NOTE ON THE TITLE

The form of Milton's title is of course common in Greek tragedy – the hero's name followed by some distinguishing word or phrase: *Oedipus the King, Oedipus at Colonnus, Prometheus Bound*, and so on. It is worth considering briefly what significance the epithet *Agonistes* may have had for Milton.

The *agonist* was a contender in the Greek games, the forerunner of the modern Olympic athlete. The word *agonistes* in Milton's title must refer primarily to Samson's physical prowess: his feats in the celebrations organised for Dagon, and his final wrestling with the pillars which upheld the 'spacious Theatre' sheltering the Philistian lords. We might paraphrase this sense by rewording the title *Samson at the Games*. It seems unlikely however, in view of Milton's general treatment of this theme, that he would have chosen a title with reference only to Samson's physical participation in Dagon's games; and tradition offers numerous examples of a symbolic extension of the idea of the athlete.

In the great period of Greek philosophy it had been suggested that the best prizes should go to those who worked hard and effectively with their minds: the *philosophical* athlete was the one who deserved best of his fellow-citizens. Then, one does not have to read very deeply in St Paul's epistles to realise that he conceived of the Christian life in terms of warfare or athletic contest: the good Christian must have his armour about him; and he must be trained (e.g. 1 Corinthians ix 24 ff.). Here the emphasis is not upon competence in abstruse thought, but rather on an athleticism of the spirit, the will and the power to engage in moral struggles. If Dr Johnson had considered *Samson Agonistes* with the Pauline idea of the Christian athlete in mind, he might have recognised that it does embody a genuinely dramatic conflict, that it is more than an empty preparation for an unmotivated catastrophe.

A further aspect of Milton's drama is suggested by the related word 'agonistic', which is a rhetorical term denoting the attempt to overcome an adversary in argument. If we compare *Samson* with any Shakesperean tragedy, we immediately notice an absence of action, or plot, in Milton's drama, and realise how much it hinges upon discussions which often become 'arguments'. Manoah, Dalila, Harapha all represent viewpoints which are, for Samson, temptations. It is not too fanciful to imagine these figures as 'internalised' and their voices expressing plausible temptations arising within Samson's own mind. If we recall Bunyan's *Grace Abounding to the Chief of Sinners*, or Richard Baxter's *Autobiography*, we shall recollect how central to the lives of these seventeenth-century Puritans was the constant wrestling with temptation, which was felt so vividly that they often described it in terms drawn from actual argument with a real opponent, or even in terms of physical conflict. One way of reading *Samson* is to follow it *as an argument*, asking oneself periodically what precisely the discussion is about, and what stage it has now reached?

Another related word is of course 'agony', and no special insight is required to see that Samson's agony, particularly his agony of mind and spirit, is quite central in Milton's presentation – so much so that many critics have been deflected by its expression to thinking about Milton's own sufferings rather than about his art. Also the word 'agony' is traditionally used in a context which some critics regard as having great relevance to Milton's conception of his hero. In Gethsemane, immediately before Christ's arrest, trial and crucifixion, he suffered 'the agony in the garden'.

'SAMSON' AND THE GREEK TRAGEDY

In the preface to *Samson Agonistes* Milton makes a general statement on 'that sort of Dramatic Poem which is call'd Tragedy'. He makes it clear that in writing his drama, he gave careful consideration both to Aristotle's classical theory of tragedy, and to actual examples of Greek drama, particularly the works of '*Aeschulus, Sophocles* and *Euripides*, the three Tragic Poets unequall'd yet by any'. The relationship of *Samson* with Greek theory and practice cannot be discussed at all fully here. Luckily it is easy to do some useful background reading, as the relevant texts are quite short. Judges xiii–xvi is the essential Biblical text, and to this one should add the Book of Job. For the classical background one should read Aristotle's *Poetics*, the *Prometheus Bound* of Aeschylus, and the *Oedipus at Colonnus* of Sophocles, all of which are easily obtainable in translation.

Structurally, *Samson* is obviously much closer to Greek tragedy than to contemporary English works; indeed it is even more regular in construction than most Greek tragedies! Milton limits the action to the final episode in Samson's life, limits the duration of the action to a few hours only, keeps Samson on stage for almost the whole time, and has the final event occur off-stage. The chorus is used in the Greek way, to provide a commentary on the action from the standpoint of the ordinary man, to point significances and sometimes to lament, to give 'flashbacks' on Samson's past career, thus rooting the drama in the Biblical story while avoiding reference to the more embarrassing episodes in Samson's career. (It is worth listing those events in Judges xiii–xvi which are *not* mentioned in *Samson*, and considering what the omissions may suggest about Milton's conception of his hero.)

'CONCENTRATION' AND MILTON'S LANGUAGE

If asked to name the most important single quality *Samson* derives from its 'Greek' construction, I should say 'concentration'. It is short enough to be read at a single sitting; there is no 'sub-plot' to complicate our response; everything has a direct relation to the hero. The language of the verse, shorn of connotative exuberance, demarcates the action like a spotlight: for the time *this* is all that matters. Some critics have objected to the poem's diction, declaring that it denies the resources of language, depriving English of its natural richness and sap. *Samson*'s language has been compared unfavourably with that of *Comus*, with little consideration for the very different kinds of decorum required by each. Defenders of *Samson*'s language have pointed to Milton's 'up-to-dateness', pointing out that Shakesperean richness in diction was generally avoided in the age of Dryden, and that this was the age when members of the Royal Society were imposing on themselves a 'close, naked, natural way of speaking'. It is interesting that the language of *Samson* can be linked with contemporary practice and aspiration in this way, but I do not think that it is critically very relevant. The austerity of Milton's language is perfectly in accord with the nature of his subject; it has the strength and honesty – and lack of superficial 'attractiveness' – of a mind purged of self-deception and compromise. Those who object to the language of *Samson* are tacitly urging the claims of the 'sensibility' which enjoys poetic language in and for itself; but the action of this drama takes place in a region where sensibility is not enough.

If 'concentration' is indeed an important quality of *Samson*, then we should try to honour the fact in the way we read it. Inevitably when studying the play we have to focus on particular parts in turn, and it may well be that less experienced readers will need to examine the parts separately before they are able to take in the work as a whole. It should be remembered though that Milton unquestionably designed the work to be read at a single sitting; and we shall not feel its peculiar intensity and power until we respond to this intention.

SAMSON
(1–114)

Our knowledge of the Biblical story enables Milton to initiate us rapidly into the physical and mental situation of his hero. We learn that the action is to deal with the last phase of Samson's career; he is already blinded, a prisoner of the Philistines, and this is to be the last day of his life:

> This day a solemn Feast the people hold
> To *Dagon* thir Sea-Idol, and forbid
> Laborious works, unwillingly this rest
> Thir Superstition yeilds me; hence with leave
> Retiring from the popular noise, I seek
> This unfrequented place to find some ease;
> Ease to the body some, none to the mind
> From restless thoughts.   (12 ff.)

The word 'agonistes' indicates not merely a combatant, but a champion. Samson, dejected as he is now, is God's champion, the arena of the combat is his own soul, and the enemy to be defeated is the 'deadly swarm' of his own thoughts. From the beginning we know the physical outcome of this action; a seventeenth-century reader would also have foretold the spiritual outcome, since in the tradition Samson had long been a hero of Christianity. The interest lies in the author's management of the internal struggle that is to transform defeat into victory. Underlying Milton's conception, besides the 'Samson' tradition and the influence of the Greeks, there is the pastoral theology of seventeenth-century Puritanism, with its emphasis on the strivings of conscience and the plausible casuistry of evil.

At various points in the work episodes from Samson's career will be recalled by the Chorus, by Manoah, by Dalila. What Samson recalls here is no particular incident illustrating his lost greatness, but the divine source of his power revealed by the angel who foretold his birth and prescribed the manner of his upbringing. Samson's predicament is that of a man who has betrayed God's plan, who has squandered his gifts through intemperance. However, the misery Samson goes on to express (30-42) is not so much that of the sinner conscious of having betrayed his God, as that of a man who has been betrayed by his wife, blinded and enslaved by his enemies. Though few of us can feel the right to say so, this is self-pity rather than contrition. The temptation to self-pity presents itself in many forms as the drama unfolds, usually resolving into the temptation to 'make the best of things' and leave God's purposes to God. The opposition to the temptation derives from Samson's sense of election; groping and blind in mind as well as in body, he can yet never accept that the easy solution is the right one. An 'agonist' opposes, and Samson struggles with the protean temptation to mental ease until he wins through to an inner fortitude at last commensurate with his physical strength.

Samson puts his complaint in the form of a question: in effect, 'Why the supernatural promises if this is how it all ends?' It would be a plausible question, but we notice that it is not posed in the spirit of intellectual enquiry. Samson neither expects nor really desires an answer: intellectual satisfaction on such a point could only offer hollow satisfaction! Samson supplies the only proper answer himself, that is, that he has no right to put the question:

> Yet stay, let me not rashly call in doubt
> Divine Prediction; what if all foretold
> Had been fulfilld but through mine own default;
> Whom have I to complain of but my self?   (43 ff.)

The brilliant sequence 'foretold... fulfilld... default' is more than merely verse splendidly written for speaking aloud. Samson has just been bitterly commenting on the disparity between his present plight and the hopes of his birth: 'There's no sense in it' is the underlying burden of those anguished questions. The burden of *this* question is that, however much it might suit him to do so, Samson cannot convict his life of being meaningless. There might be sense in it, however bitter a sense: the possible relation between his *default* and the failure of what had been *foretold* is not hard to see. There is no comfort in it for Samson, and there is no incongruity in his passing over into further lamentation; but the 'agonist' has won the first of many tiny victories. Though he experiences himself as a broken reject, he recognises the existence of order and justice.

Of course we must not take this acknowledgement of divine justice out of context, overstress it, and produce a Samson regenerate from the beginning. The admission of personal responsibility is only a moment in a lengthy utterance; but it does mark the beginning of the struggle which is to end in victory. The current of personal feeling runs strongly on as Samson recalls the humiliating surrender to Dalila which occasioned his downfall. The next reference to the divine will (60–3) is perhaps stronger than the first. Does Samson's reference to the inscrutability of providence indicate a belief that God may still be able to use him? I think not. If the reader takes it as glancing at the path along which Samson's 'dark steps' may be led, he must accept the statement as belonging to that species of dramatic irony in which the protagonist speaks very much more than he knows. Again, it is only a moment in a lengthy utterance, and Samson goes on to give passionate and lyrical expression to his feelings, in a passage which rises to a sense of cosmic deprivation:

> The Sun to me is dark
> And silent as the Moon,
> When she deserts the night
> Hid in her vacant interlunar cave.   (86 ff.)

One is reminded of the famous cry of Pascal: 'The silence of the eternal spaces terrifies me.'

SAMSON AND THE CHORUS
(115–330)

Whereas through Samson's own eyes we have seen the contrast between his divinely ordained birth and upbringing and his present plight, through the eyes of the Chorus we have a more 'external' view. They emphasise the contrast between what he now looks like physically, 'with languisht head unpropt,' and the 'irresistible Samson' of earlier days, 'whom unarmd / No strength of man, or fiercest wild beast could withstand'. They speak of him tearing the lion, working havoc with the jawbone of a dead ass, removing the gates of Azza. And, as people do in the presence of misfortune, they go on to philosophise about it. In fact, they generalise from Samson's case to construct a theory of tragedy, for that is what is quite clearly implied in lines 164–75. As G. and M. Bullough comment, 'Samson is not just the medieval tragic hero cast down by Fortune, but the Aristotelian hero ruined by a moral flaw' (*Milton's Dramatic Poems* 203). If the theory is Aristotelian, it is also modern in its insistence that it is human potentialities and weaknesses which make a tragic hero, rather than something fortuitous like being a king.

Samson's first words to the Chorus (187 ff.) apparently – but only apparently – contradict what he has earlier said (66 ff.) about the loss of his sight:

> Yet that which was the worst now least afflicts me,
> Blindness, for had I sight, confus'd with shame,
> How could I once look up, or heave the head. (195 ff.)

Psychologically, the movement is entirely natural. Previously Samson had been immersed in himself; now his mind moves outwards, and as he imagines his situation in the eyes of his people, he is filled with shame. It is a painful moment, but represents a necessary step towards his regeneration, a turning towards renewed fellowship with his own people. At first the shame is more than he can bear, and he retreats by implying a condemnation of God for giving him strength without wisdom (206 ff.). However plausible Samson's words are psychologically, what they imply is unacceptable. The task God had set him was not too hard for his intelligence; it merely required common prudence; and, if we recall the Biblical story, Samson had plenty of warning of the Philistines' intentions before he finally succumbed to Dalila.

The reply of the Chorus is very human, embracing a Jewish commonplace (Don't call God into question); a universal cliché (Many wise men have been deceived by women); and something like vulgar curiosity (But why did you do it?).

In putting into Samson's mouth the answer to this last question, of why he had married a woman of the Philistines, Milton makes a subtle and significant point (219 ff.). Samson explains, of his first marriage, to the woman of Timna, that he knew 'From intimat impulse' that the marriage was God's will. This was, of course, an excellent reason. We must rely

Samson and the Chorus

upon, as we must obey, the inner light. Old Testament prophets and seventeenth-century Puritans agree on that. Yet the responsibility is an awful one; for nothing is easier than to mistake the promptings of our own unregenerate natures for the inward call from God. T. S. Eliot has reminded us that sex, the most imperative of the instincts, 'may simulate to perfection the voice of the Holy Spirit' ('Thoughts after Lambeth'). That is what happened to Samson, as he confesses:

> ... the next I took to Wife
> (O that I never had! fond wish too late)
> Was in the Vale of *Sorec, Dalila*,
> That specious Monster, my accomplisht snare.
> I thought it lawful from my former act,
> And the same end; still watching to oppress
> *Israels* oppressours.' (227 ff.)

The next (brief) speech of the Chorus (237–40) takes up Samson's words 'still watching to oppress / *Israels* oppressours'. Psychologically it is very natural. It says the kind of thing we are all apt to say to someone to whom we are trying to be kind, but toward whom we have an underlying hostility. It begins with balm and ends with gall: 'Yet *Israel* still serves with all his Sons.'

It is important to recognise the underlying significance of Samson's long reply (241–76). The clear implication of the Chorus's words is that '*Israel* still serves with all his Sons' because Samson, for all his perseverance in hostility toward the Philistines, was an ineffectual champion for Israel. (There is also a possible suggestion that Samson was simply deluded in his belief that God had especially chosen him.) Samson's reply shows that he has lost neither his common sense nor his sense of his own dignity. There are two extremes of response possible in a plight such as Samson's. He could have said 'It is all their fault' ('they' being Dalila, Israel's governors and so on). Such a response would probably be termed 'paranoid,' and, as we have seen, Samson avoids this: he has already blamed himself, admitted a good deal of personal responsibility in the matter. The other extreme would be to say 'It is all my fault'. Perhaps there are few situations in life where it is true to say 'It is *all* my fault'; at all events Samson's is not one of them.

Either extreme response would be a sign of psychic collapse, but Samson is not so broken in spirit that he is willing to say either 'It is all their fault' or 'It is all my fault.' He is sufficiently self-possessed to be able to distinguish what is his fault and what is not; and he retains sufficient 'self-esteem, grounded on just and right' (*PL* VIII 572), to want to distinguish.

We may read this speech (241–76) as a rebuke to the Chorus for its implied 'ingratitude' for Samson's 'worthiest deeds' (276). The Chorus here stands for the whole Israelite nation, who had failed to understand – and therefore to rightly act upon – the deeds of God done through Samson. The end of this speech, from 265 on, has been read as Milton's rebuke to the English nation for preferring the 'bondage with ease' of Charles II's rule to the 'strenuous liberty' of the Commonwealth. Such a reading is not so much incorrect as irrelevant, and dangerously irrelevant in so far as it leads our attention away from the inner drama of Milton's tragedy. It is only when we are conscious of *Samson* as being inwardly dramatic that we can escape the force of Johnson's criticism that 'the intermediate parts have neither cause nor consequence, neither hasten nor retard the catastrophe' (*Life of Milton*). This will ring true if we have no idea of dramatic action beyond external event; but *Samson* is a drama of *internal* event. It is a play about spiritual rebirth, and we begin to perceive its truly dramatic nature when we read it with sufficient care and sympathy to register, in Samson's successive speeches, the slow, struggling

Samson and the Chorus

process of his regeneration. Here, the clean, firm summary of the relevant history which Samson utters, by way of rebutting the implication that he is to blame for Israel's continued slavery, – his quiet confidence in the justice of what he says, signals a moral firmness and intellectual clarity which is far from what we would have inferred from the Chorus's first description of Samson lying

> ... at random, carelessly diffus'd,
> With languisht head unpropt,
> As one past hope, abandond,
> And by himself giv'n over.   (118 ff.)

It is perhaps relevant here to recall the famous passage in *Areopagitica* on the relationship between temptation and virtue (*SM* 738): it is by resisting temptation that we become virtuous. Here the Chorus, Manoah, Dalila and Harapha represent temptations of different kinds. The Chorus's description of Samson, which I have just quoted, was not inaccurate. Samson did indeed feel very much as he looked; and clearly the most pressing danger of such a condition is a collapse into total, undistinguishing despair and self-abasement. We may read the Chorus's speech (237–40) as representing a perhaps unconscious invitation to Samson to despair completely. Spenser, whom Milton thought 'a better teacher than Scotus or Aquinas', had represented Despair as one of the most seductive of temptations (in *The Faerie Queene* I ix). Samson's reply (241–76) represents a victory over that temptation.

The Chorus's next speech (277–89) is rather clotted with Biblical reference, and some explanation is called for. *Succoth* and *Penuel* refused to give bread to *Gideon*, when he was pursuing the vanquished kings of *Madian*. Later he punished them (Judges viii 4–17). *Jephtha* was rejected by his own people (Judges xi 2) because he was the son of a harlot (the 'argument' Milton refers to occurs in Judges xi 4–28). The argument was not accepted by the Ammonites, so Jephtha made a vow unto the Lord (Judges xi 31) and then beat the Ammonites in battle. (As a result of the vow he had to sacrifice his daughter, thus becoming an example of one of God's champions who suffered rejection by his people *and* did the hard, right thing toward God. Afterwards Israel's girls lamented Jephtha's daughter four days in every year.) The men of Ephraim were angry that Jephtha had fought the Ammonites without enlisting their help; Jephtha therefore gathered together the men of Gilead and successfully fought the Ephraimites: 'fourtie and two thousand' were slain. Those trying to escape by passing themselves off as *not* being Ephraimites were asked to pronounce *Shibboleth*, which the Ephraimites could not pronounce properly, saying *Sibboleth*. The passage in *Samson* is difficult partly because readers tend to be confused by the fact that the plural ('thir pride': 286) refers back to the generic singular ('*Ephraim*': 282). The problem here is whether we should take these Biblical references as referring solely to their immediate context in *Samson*, or whether they have an anticipatory significance (see the chapter 'Milton's Similes' in my Critical Commentary on *Paradise Lost*). One probably relevant piece of information is that in Christian iconography Gideon and Jephtha, like Samson himself and like Job, are considered to be prototypes of Christ; but not all prototypes were equal: Job, for example, was usually considered to be the fullest prototype. It is interesting to notice a possible connection here with the great friend of Milton's youth, Charles Diodati. Charles had an uncle, also named Diodati, with whom Milton spent some time during his European tour; this uncle published an annotated Bible, and it is clear from this that in comparison with Gideon and

Samson and the Chorus

Jephtha he regarded Samson as being a very special prototype of Christ. To consider this problem fully we should need to know in some detail what it was about Gideon, Jephtha and Samson that made commentators regard them as foreshadowing Christ; and I confess that even after some study of the matter I do not feel confident. But this is certain: if we consider the references to be anticipatory, without taking into account possible allegorical interpretations, we shall end up with a literalist interpretation and floundering in the biographical fallacy. Gideon and Jephtha deserved well of their countrymen, but were badly treated by them (and Milton might well have thought in similar terms of himself). Gideon and Jephtha both turned upon their countrymen, whereas Samson did not; but those who like to interpret *Samson* biographically love to see it as a threat by the aged, blind, and politically defeated Milton towards the Restoration régime. If we take the Chorus's passage both proleptically and literally we may well see that it is concealing such a threat on Milton's part.

The immediately relevant point is that Gideon and Jephtha, like Samson, deserved better of their countrymen than they received. Interpreting the Chorus psychologically, we may see it as an admission of the truth of what Samson has just said (241–76) and as an attempted diversion. Samson, in rebutting the implication that it is solely his fault that '*Israel* still serves with all his Sons', comes too close to home for the Chorus's comfort; they reply by saying in effect 'Yes, you are right, and this kind of thing has happened before', reverting to Gideon and Jephtha as examples which they can contemplate with greater mental comfort because of their historical remoteness. (Gideon and Jephtha might not in fact have been so remote from the Israelites of Samson's time; but for Milton's audience, who have Samson before their eyes, they are.)

Perhaps we are wrong to look for complexity and anticipatory significance at this point. The examples given by the Chorus, by the very fact that they do not fully agree with Samson's case, emphasise the fact that Samson is special. His story is going to end differently from theirs. But dramatic irony is at work here; for Samson does not know this yet. Therefore he is content to make a third in the series Gideon–Jephtha–Samson: 'Of such examples add mee to the roul' (290). He does not yet know that God will enable him to transcend these predecessors. He does know that while his people may easily neglect him (as the people of Succoth and Penuel were ungrateful to Gideon and those of Ephraim to Jephtha) they cannot afford to neglect 'God's propos'd deliverance' (292). We may regard Samson's reply (290–2) as a threat, uttered ostensibly on God's behalf but actually indicating Samson's ill-suppressed desire for revenge on his own people (as John Broadbent appears to: p. 45), but this seems a strained interpretation.

The final speech of the Chorus in this section (293–325) is perhaps best read as a somewhat bewildered comment on the strangeness of the affair, combined with a determination not to call God into question. This speech seems deliberately low-keyed and somewhat meandering to contrast with the firmness and clarity of Samson's preceding long speech (241–76). It evokes memories of the book of Job, in which doubts about God's justice are answered. In 210–17 the Chorus had begun by telling Samson not to 'tax divine disposal', but had ended on a note of doubt as to why Samson had married outside his own nation. Here, one notices, Samson has arrived at a position which seems to square with that of the ordinary orthodox religious man, so the Chorus begins by apparently echoing what he has said. It is amusing to notice how they end, back at the 'problem' of the woman of Timna. One is not sure how seriously to take the Chorus at this point; my own feeling is that Milton is not fully to be identified with what John Broadbent calls the logic-chopping about the woman of Timna (though doubtless a seventeenth-century Puritan as well as an Old Testament Israelite would have been 'stained' if he had married an unchaste woman). We are too cocksurely post-Freudian if we imagine that Milton cannot have been sardonically amused at the degree of interest shown by the Chorus in Samson's sex-life!

SAMSON AND MANOAH
(326–651)

The words of the Chorus to this point have been those of Samson's own countrymen, loyal to him but somewhat ambivalent in their attitude, showing occasionally flashes of the cruelty which seems to lie close to pity within the human mind. Manoah, Samson's own father, exhibits an even wider range of response. If *Samson* is a play about heroism, it is also a play about the fact that we are all members one of another. The hero's contact with his fellow-countrymen, uncertain as they have been in their comprehension, was yet a healing contact. Samson's contact with his own father is to mark another advance toward his regeneration, even though he receives as an astringent what Manoah offers as balm.

Samson is a stern and terrible drama; but this should not blind us to the manifestations of ordinary humanity within it, which, by contrast with the prevailing mood, verge on the quietly humorous. There is a platitudinous obviousness about Manoah which should evoke an affectionate response even while the drama is educating us to reject, as Samson rejects, the temptation he offers. That temptation may be summed up in his name, which means 'rest'.

In his first speech (340–72) Manoah progresses from platitude ('O ever failing trust / In mortal strength': 348) to apparent impiety: God has treated Samson over-harshly (368–72). Arnold Stein suggests that it is easy to misjudge Manoah at this point, and reminds us of the 'family relationship' between the Jews and God: 'He is transgressing and, I conjecture, he knows that God knows it, and that this is the grief of the father Manoa speaking, and not the piety of the son Manoa.' The point is an interesting one, though I cannot feel sufficiently sure of Milton's understanding of Hebraism to assess whether it accurately reflects his intention. At all events, the psychological movement of Manoah's speech is natural: the evocation of Samson's warlike prowess (340–5) shows a residual paternal pride, and a slightly impious pride at that, since Manoah does not talk of God's strength in Samson. Naturally, yet nevertheless impiously, it is his fatherhood of Samson that most nearly touches him, not God's fatherhood of them both. And with his pity for his son is mingled pity for himself, as of one deluded by God into great expectations. The regeneration of the hero, in which we may discern the principle drama of *Samson*, is educative for the hero's people, – and, by extension, for the reader. At the close of the action the hero's father gives expression to what it has had to teach us.

At line 210 the Chorus said to Samson, 'Tax not divine disposal'. At that moment Samson had been making a point similar to the one Manoah makes at the end of his first speech, except that Samson implied a doubt of God's wisdom and Manoah implies one about his mercy. Samson's reply to Manoah, in which he places the blame for his present sufferings squarely and fully upon his own past follies, indicates another step forward in his regeneration.

It is worth noticing the exact language in which Samson takes the blame upon himself: 'I my self have brought them on, / Sole Author I, sole cause' (375). Samson here takes to himself two words which were often applied to God. God is the 'sole author' and 'sole cause' of the physical universe and of all life. Yet he cannot be blamed for the evil in the universe, — a point which Milton is at pains to make in *Paradise Lost*. God, in giving man free will, gives him a creative responsibility for the way he lives his life. Samson's recital of his follies carries on by implication the logic of this admission: his wives betrayed him, but could not have done so if he had not first betrayed God's secret. The ending of this speech, in which Samson recognises that his present state of (enforced) slavery is not so ignominious as the (voluntary) slavery of his relationship with his wives, recalls a striking phrase from the *Doctrine and Discipline of Divorce*, in which Milton described the unhappily married man as 'grinding in the mill of a servile copulation' (*SM 586*).

At this point one feels that Samson is seeing with an almost unbearable passionate clarity. The mental blindness which had led to his physical blinding has been dispelled; but in any distressing situation, prolonged in extent, it is easier to contemplate those past actions which are responsible for the situation than to contemplate the evil that is still to come. To make sense of our past is essential, and nobody would wish to belittle the spiritual progress Samson has made so far; but to overcome our bondage to circumstance we must take the further and more difficult step of acting responsibly in order to shape the future. Manoah's next speech (420–47) forces Samson to realise that the consequences of his folly have not, even yet, worked themselves out. (The realisation that he may still have a part to play does not, however, come until later.)

Samson was of course already aware that the Philistines were to hold a feast to Dagon. Manoah now makes him aware that he is in a sense to feature in the festivities (though he will not be aware of how fully the Philistines intend him to feature until the arrival of the Officer). The feast is being held to praise Dagon 'as thir God who hath delivered / Thee *Samson* bound and blind into thir hands' (437). In the way Manoah conveys this information we may discern a complex of motives: his piety as a Hebrew is outraged by the thought of the Philistine's triumph; his sense of his standing in his community is degraded by the thought that his own son is responsible. The injury to his self-esteem is in exact proportion to his earlier pride in being the father of one chosen by God. It is not surprising that the facts of the matter are conveyed as reproach:

> Which to have come to pass by means of thee,
> *Samson*, of all thy sufferings think the heaviest,
> Of all reproach the most with shame that ever
> Could have befall'n thee and thy Fathers house.
>
> (444 ff.)

In reply (448–71) Samson acknowledges and confesses the justice of Manoah's accusation. We feel that in his acknowledgement Samson has more dignity than his father: it is a confession of personal fault which is purged of all irrelevant consciousness of self. By contrast, Manoah's dignity is somewhat imperilled by his nagging consciousness that it is *his* son, *his* family; a proper appraisal of the situation would not throw the personal so much into the foreground. Manoah's concentration on his own emotional stake in the Philistine's triumph involves an obscuring of his faith, in spite of the orthodox reference to 'God, / Besides whom is no God' (440). It is therefore left to Samson to point out that God 'will arise and his great name assert' (467); to point out, in fact, that while he has failed and must suffer for his failure, God is not in the last resort dependent upon man. The very

Samson and Manoah

fact that God's champion has been overthrown indicates the imminence of God's overthrow of his enemies; at this point we are meant to understand that while Manoah speaks with the language of orthodoxy, Samson sees with the eye of faith.

One feels that there is comfort for Samson in dismissing himself from the reckoning, and anticipating God's triumph over Dagon. He is beyond the reach of ordinary human comfort; and indeed when Manoah would press it upon him he is driven to despair. Humanly speaking, Samson is wrecked. He has come to terms with the fact. Yet he retains something of a champion's spirit, so that he cannot bear the thought of what would be involved in Manoah's proposed salvage-operation. What, to most people's vision, would stand for a peacefully sedentary old age, is unbearable for Samson to contemplate:

> To what can I be useful, wherein serve
> My Nation, and the work from Heav'n imposed,
> But to sit idle on the houshold hearth,
> A burdenous drone; to visitants a gaze,
> Or pitied object, these redundant locks
> Robustious to no purpose clustring down,
> Vain monument of strength; till length of years
> And sedentary numness craze my limbs
> To a contemptible old age obscure. (564 ff.)

It is a merely rhetorical question. Samson, in his terms, the terms of a champion, can no longer be useful. He has quietly admitted as much (460). But resignation to God's terms is not resignation to Manoah's. The vision of uselessness conjured up by Manoah's proposal wrings from Samson a cry which tells us, the readers, that he still wants to be useful. Born and raised a hero, he can think only in heroic terms. Manoah's attempt to comfort him (577–89) is too facile; it cannot raise any genuine hope. Samson's desire for usefulness, confronting the apparent impossibility of its fulfilment, brings him to a more exquisite agony of despair than he has so far expressed, an agony which can be expressed only in terms of the most extreme physical pain:

> Thoughts my Tormenters armd with deadly stings
> Mangle my apprehensive tenderest parts,
> Exasperate, exulcerate, and raise
> Dire inflammation. (623 ff.)

CHORUS
(652–709)

We shall understand this Chorus better if we follow up a hint in its opening lines:

> Many are the sayings of the wise
> In ancient and in modern books inrould;
> Extolling Patience as the truest fortitude.
> (652 ff.)

We may understand from this that there is more than one kind of fortitude, patience being the truest; and that the point has been discussed by ancient and modern philosophers. This is in fact the case. From the Stoic philosophers down through the Christian centuries there had been discussion of the role of patience in the ethical and religious life. It had been classified as a kind of fortitude, the other kind being often described as magnanimity. St Thomas Aquinas, in discussing 'fortitude', described magnanimity as a virtue of aggression and patience as a virtue of endurance ('Treatise on Fortitude' in *Summa Theologica*, London, 1922 (Part II, Second Part, qu. CXXIII–CXXXIX)). In his *Apologie for Poetrie* (1595) Sir Philip Sidney writes that the trials of Ulysses are but 'exercises of patience and magnanimity'. We may say that magnanimity is the kind of fortitude appropriate to the hero of epic, patience the kind appropriate to the Christian saint. There can be little doubt which of the two Milton preferred to celebrate in his verse. In the famous Prologue to Book IX of *Paradise Lost* he describes himself as:

> Not sedulous by Nature to indite
> Warrs, hitherto the onely Argument
> Heroic deemd, chief maistrie to dissect
> With long and tedious havoc fabl'd Knights
> In Battels feignd; the better fortitude
> Of Patience and Heroic Martyrdom
> Unsung. (*PL* IX 27 ff.)

At the end of *Paradise Lost* Adam has learned 'that suffering for Truths sake / Is fortitude to highest victorie' (*PL* XII 569); – and of course etymologically 'patience' is equivalent to 'suffering'.

Two more facts from the historical treatment of the virtue of patience are pertinent, one to the stress Milton intends in *Samson Agonistes*, the other to the question of why this particular chorus is placed where it is in the drama. First, it is useful to know that in the Middle Ages and the Renaissance the Samson legend played a part in iconographic representations of the virtue of patience. For example, in *The Florentine Fior di Virtu* (1491) there is a chapter on the dual aspect of fortitude which is illustrated by a woodcut of Samson pulling down the temple (and indeed, when one thinks of it, this is wonderfully emblematic of an action which is also a suffering!). This should lead us to suspect that 'patience' is important in Milton's conception of Samson. The second thing to note is that in Christian times 'fortitude' came to be thought of as the safeguard against the deadly sin of 'despair', the temptation to which Samson seems in danger of succumbing at this point:

'Nor am I in the list of them that hope; / Hopeless are all my evils, all remediless' (647). In Spenser's *The Faerie Queene* (I x 21) it was at the very point where 'the faithfull knight' had grown to 'perfection of all heavenly grace' that he was so

> Greevd with remembrance of his wicked wayes,
> And prickt with anguish of his sinnes so sore,
> That he desirde, to end his wretched dayes:
> So much the dart of sinfull guilt the soule dismayes.

(It is interesting, when we are considering *Samson*, and when we recall Milton's avowed admiration for Spenser as a moral teacher, to notice that Spenser sees despair as a temptation of those who have 'grown to perfection of all heavenly grace'.) And it is at this point, just when 'remembrance of his wicked wayes' leads him to desire death, that he is cured of his despair by – Patience:

> a Leach, the which had great insight
> In that disease of grieved conscience,
> And well could cure the same; His name was *Patience*.
> *(FQ* I x 23)

The foregoing should help us to see why it is at this point that the Chorus should speak of 'Patience, the truest fortitude'; but even though we have grounds for believing that Milton accepted this traditional doctrine of Christian ethics, we should not conclude that the Chorus is here merely echoing Milton's feelings, or that Milton is inserting Christian sentiment in a propagandist rather than a dramatic way. In fact, if we read the whole Chorus carefully, we see that the Danites are by no means delivering a homily on patience. While at the end of the Chorus they pray to God on Samson's behalf, through much of its length they empathise with Samson's mental sufferings. Their words show that they are aware of the importance traditionally ascribed to the virtue of patience; but not until the tragedy is accomplished does the traditional teaching become real to them. Their need to learn that patience is indeed the 'truest fortitude' is hinted at in lines 1268–96, where the tone of lines 1268–86 reveals that their emotional preference is for magnanimity (Aquinas's 'virtue of aggression') rather than for patience. As so often in *Paradise Lost* (and indeed in *Comus*) the writing shows that Milton realises the attractiveness of what he condemns. (The reader will find this point, which I take to be central to an understanding of Milton's strategy as a poet 'doctrinal to a nation', dealt with more largely in my Critical Commentary on *Paradise Lost* and Critical Commentary on Milton's *Comus and Shorter Poems*.)

Commentaries on this Chorus (651–710) frequently refer to the history of Milton's own time, with the implication that he is here obliquely reviling the Restoration régime. It may well be that the fate of the Commonwealth for which he had worked was in his mind when he wrote lines 687–704. If *Samson* was, as is generally believed, written after the Restoration, Milton could hardly have written these lines *without* thinking of the 'change of times' which England had so recently suffered; of the heads of Cromwell, Bradshaw and Ireton, placed on poles on the top of Westminster Hall for several years, 'to fowls a prey'; of himself suffering from the gout, the drunkard's disease afflicting the abstemious, 'causless suffering / The punishment of dissolute days'. It is right and proper that modern commentators should remind us of facts which were probably in Milton's mind when he wrote this passage; but we should be wary of assuming that we now 'understand' the lines because we are in possession of such facts. If we leave it there, we are putting certain particulars in place of a statement which is rather generalised – which is certainly comprehensible without those particulars, and which would still have its validity if Cromwell's body had not been disinterred and dishonoured, and if Milton in old age had not suffered from gout. History could still offer numerous examples of the same class of events. The point is that Milton is making a statement of general validity; we falsify his intention if we see the passage in terms of any *one* set of particulars. The point is worth dwelling on, because naturally annotators of Milton or of any other author like to present us with facts. This is legitimate and useful; but it is dangerously easy for us then to make a step which is illegitimate and to begin to 'interpret' his work in biographical terms. Milton's imagination is such that the 'facts' in his works are always placed in a larger historical and ethical framework: it is the relation of particulars to this framework which should concern us as readers.

SAMSON AND DALILA
(710–1009)

Our first view of Dalila is brilliantly managed:

> But who is this, what thing of Sea or Land?
> Femal of sex it seems,
> That so bedeckt, ornate, and gay,
> Comes this way sailing
> Like a stately Ship
> Of *Tarsus*, bound for th' Iles
> Of *Javan* or *Gadier*
> With all her bravery on, and tackle trim,
> Sails filld, and streamers waving,
> Courted by all the winds that hold them play,
> An Amber sent of odorous perfume
> Her harbinger, a damsel train behind;
> Some rich *Philistian* Matron she may seem,
> And now at nearer view, no other certain
> Then *Dalila* thy wife. (710–24)

Few people would accuse Milton of 'intermixing Comic

Samson and Dalila

stuff with tragic sadness and gravity ... corruptly to gratifie the people' (see his Preface to *Samson, Of that sort of Dramatic Poem which is call'd Tragedy*).

Yet the tone of this is comic, and obviously affects our response to Dalila. Milton is a master of this particular kind of description, in which an (at first unspecified) object comes into clearer focus. Here Dalila is at first only a 'thing', only 'seems' 'Femal of sex'. As she comes closer, we notice that her scent is strong enough to be smelled – and recognised – before her identity is established. Perhaps it is super-subtle to recall that in Milton's time amber was thought to be the sperm of a whale, and that the whale was traditionally associated with Satan (see *PL* I, 200 ff. and my Critical Commentary on *Paradise Lost*, pp. 75–6). If Milton did intend us to recall these things, then the image suggests a truly diabolical sexuality in Dalila.

Milton is probably observing 'decorum, which is the grand masterpiece to observe' in making the Danites employ the ship simile in reference to Dalila. The Israelites were not a seagoing nation, but some of their enemies were. We may remember also certain descriptions of Satan in *Paradise Lost* (e.g. II 636 ff.), and the fact that in earlier literature the overdressed woman is frequently compared to a fully rigged ship. Perhaps authors were aware of the possible pun in St Paul's advice to husbands (1 Thessalonians iv 4)!

This lengthy introduction to Dalila contrasts with the abruptness of Samson's response to it: 'My Wife, my Traitress, let her not come near me.' If the Danites can afford to be flippant, Samson cannot; and as if in response to his distress, the Chorus modulates into a less obtruding tone, as it describes how Dalila stands 'with head declin'd / Like a fair flower surcharg'd with dew'. The tender sensuousness of this is perfectly judged: temptation would not be temptation if it were not very attractive, and Eve was flowerlike at her fall (*PL* IX 430 ff.).

After the Chorus's description of Dalila's approach, we cannot take her altogether seriously. Her own description of herself ('With doubtful feet and wavering resolution') scarcely fits the eyewitnesses' account of her 'With all her bravery on, and tackle trim, / Sails filld, and streamers waving' (717). Yet this is not a reason for believing that she does not take herself seriously. If *Samson* is about the hero's discovery of the morality involved in being 'God's champion', it may be too that one of the themes of this episode is the discovery by Dalila, and the consequent definition for the reader, of *her* morality.

The necessary prelude to forgiveness is repentance; and the argument that Samson should have forgiven Dalila and accepted her does not take account of the fact that Dalila does not unreservedly repent. This can be seen very early, before Samson has spoken to her. She *says* that she merits Samson's displeasure, *says* that she is 'without excuse' (734), yet immediately begins to extenuate her fault ('the fact more evil drew / In the perverse event than I foresaw': 736); before she finally leaves Samson the excuses are multiplied, and indeed practically erected into justifications. With Samson's 'I myself have brought them on, / Sole Author I, sole cause' (375–6), we may compare Dalila's dispersal of her 'weakness' among all her sex (773–7) and her argument that Samson was more at fault than she was, and should therefore forgive her (778–9).

Dalila's account of her dealings with 'the Magistrates / And Princes of my countrey' (850) is plausible. There seems no particular reason for us to prefer Samson's view that she betrayed him through her inability to resist '*Philistian* gold' to her statement that 'to the public good / Privat respects must yeild' (867). Some readers may wish to side with Dalila here, and ask why, when Samson married a Philistian woman with hostile intent toward her people ('still watching to oppress / *Israels* oppressours': 232), it was so wicked of her to co-

Samson and Dalila

operate with the Magistrates and Princes of her country in the way she did. (One does not need to read far into the annals of counter-espionage to realise that governments nearer home to us than the ancient Philistines have employed women in rather similar ways.) Much of the answer is given explicitly by Samson (871–902):

(1) Samson loved her and therefore presumably intended her no harm, whereas her 'patriotism' involved her in directly harming her husband (876 ff.).

(2) He employed no deceit when he married her, made no pretence of having abandoned his hostility to her nation (884).

(3) A wife marrying outside her nation takes the nationality of her husband (and therefore Dalila did *not* owe allegiance to the Philistines (885)).

(4) If her nation chose to ignore the well-established custom (referred to in (3) above), then it acted impiously and illegally, and should not have been obeyed (888 ff.).

(5) The gods of the Philistines could not be genuine gods, if they needed to employ ungodly deeds; and were therefore to be rejected (895 ff.).

If we accept, as of course we must, the convention that the wife owes allegiance to her husband's country, all this is logical; and if Dalila had been more amenable to logic, she could not have so complacently looked forward to her future fame 'In *Ecron, Gaza, Asdod*, and in *Gath*' (981). It seems to me that our assent to Samson's statement of the ethical principles involved by no means depends upon an inert acceptance of the fact that Samson's God is the true God, and those of Dalila false.

It is perhaps worth going on to ask how it is that Samson is apparently able, in a 'good' cause, to break the laws of his nation, laws presumably acceptable to his God. Why is it that he does not come under the same sort of condemnation that he applies to the actions of Dalila? I think that at the heart of the answer to this question is Milton's view that the individual may be especially chosen and inspired by God. The Puritan insistence on the validity of the 'inner light' led many men in Milton's time into ridiculous excesses of fanaticism, such as Samuel Butler satirised in *Hudibras*. These excesses should not blind us to the centrality and the dignity of the doctrine of the inner light in Puritan thinking; or of its place in the history behind the high importance we now place upon the individual. Milton certainly believed that it is open to a man to decide for himself what is right and wrong, and to act upon those beliefs. It was his refusal to accept the laws of nation and Church without question which makes his treatise *Of Christian Doctrine* so 'advanced' a document in certain respects that, although our laws have been changing in the direction he indicated, they have not caught up with him after three hundred years. However, to proceed in this manner will not bring us closer to the poem, which dramatises Milton's firm beliefs about the relationships between individuals, society and God.

As I have indicated, we should not gloss over the ethical issue between Samson and Dalila by inertly accepting that Samson's God is the true God, and Dagon a false god. We must ask what this means, in practical terms, within the action as Milton presents it. It was Samson who claimed the right to override national custom because of an 'intimat impulse' (223), Samson who claimed, in spite of his own nation's repudiation of him, that he was not a 'private person' but one 'rais'd / With strength sufficient and command from Heav'n / To free my Countrey' (1211). The relationship between Samson and his God imposed considerable strain on his relationship with his country. In contrast, it seemed that Dalila was able to serve *her* god in a manner totally harmonious with her service to the

Samson and Dalila

'Magistrates / And Princes' (850) of her country. We may say that Philistia was a 'totalitarian' country, in which the ethical ideals imposed by its religion were held to be fully embodied in its lay authorities, so that for the individual citizen submission to the state must be submission to the highest good. The good of Dagon *is* the good of Philistia, and is to be known by consulting, not the individual conscience, but the Magistrates and Princes! When any state claims to embody absolute ethical principles, then any gods it claims to worship are indeed 'idols', since they have no genuine transcendence. The ethical principle dramatised here in the contrast between Samson's morality and that of Dalila was central to Milton's puritanism, and was the driving force of his activity as a political pamphleteer. State-imposed religious conformity was anathema to him, whether it was imposed by Laud under a monarchy or by the Presbyterians of the Westminster Assembly (see the sonnet 'Because you have thrown of your prelate Lord', discussed in my Critical Commentary on *Comus and Shorter Poems*, p. 108). It was anathema because it implicitly denied the right of the individual to his own truth. It is this right on which Samson takes his stand. The contrast between the 'institutionalized morality' of Philistia, so vividly realised in Dalila's account of her dealings with the Magistrates and Princes, and the morality of Samson's trust in the 'living God' (1140), is, I take it, vital to our interpretation of this scene. If we fail to realise its significance we are forced back into supposing, as some critics do, that Milton's primary purpose in this episode is to show Samson's newly acquired powers of resistance to sexual temptation. It is true, of course, that Dalila does discreetly remind Samson that 'though sight be lost, / Life yet hath many solaces, enjoy'd / Where other senses want not their delights' (914 ff.); and that the Chorus makes the point that

>   beauty, though injurious, hath strange power,
>   After offence returning, to regain
>   Love once possest, nor can be easily
>   Repulst, without much inward passion felt
>   And secret sting of amorous remorse.   (1003 ff.)

Nevertheless, it is my opinion that those critics who argue that Samson refuses to allow Dalila to touch his hand because he is terrified of succumbing once again to her sexual charms, interpret over-zealously. Schematically, Dalila may represent an intensification of temptation (because whereas Manoah had offered ease she offers ease plus sensuality); but this fact is not conveyed – as Milton certainly knew how to convey it – in the actual writing. There is, for example, no analogue here to lines 606–51. Samson is obviously not moved in the same way. What is important is the fierce light Samson directs on to the plausible morality that has rationalised, and continues to rationalise, so many crimes against humanity. In the reflection of that light the doctrines of private inspiration and acceptance of personal responsibility become clearly defined.

We are still left, of course, with the 'problem' of Dalila's motives. I am inclined to agree with Arnold Stein in thinking that Milton's presentation of her character adds up to a portrait of *power-hunger*; and this is certainly how Samson sees her: 'How wouldst thou insult / When I must live uxorious to thy will / In perfet thraldom' (944).

CHORUS
(1010–60)

The 'biographical fallacy' has loomed large in commentaries on this section. Critics have reminded us of Milton's first marriage and gone on to assume that the low opinion of women expressed here is a direct intrusion of Milton's views into his

Chorus

drama. Warburton believed that Milton chose Samson as a subject 'for the sake of the satire on bad wives'. Milton's nineteenth-century biographer, David Masson, says of lines 1010–45 that they sum up Milton's 'incurably perverted opinion of women'. Even so intelligent a twentieth-century commentator as F. T. Prince speculates about the 'personal inspiration' of Milton's eloquence in this Chorus.

The error of this kind of 'criticism', so common in the nineteenth century, has received a good deal of attention from recent theorists of literature; moreover it was pointed out clearly enough by Milton himself. In his *Apology for Smectymnuus* (1642) he insisted that 'the author is ever distinguished from the person he introduces'; and in the *Defensio Prima* (1651) he wrote: 'One must not regard the poet's words as his own, but consider what person in the play speaks... such words are put into their mouths as is most fitting for each character, not such as the poet would speak if he were speaking in his own person.'

Milton's attitude to women was much more reasonable than remarks such as those by Warburton and Masson would suggest, as I have pointed out in the section 'Man and Woman' in my Critical Commentary on *Paradise Lost*. However, I am concerned here not to do justice to Milton as a man, but to stress that if we pay genuine attention to this Chorus, and consider it as a moment in a drama, we shall not feel impelled to gossip about Milton as a private individual. When we think of this Chorus's position in the drama, two things become quite clear: firstly, that it is entirely natural for the Chorus, just after the departure of Dalila, to talk about women and their relationship with men; secondly, that it would be strange indeed if at this point the Chorus had been full of compliments about women. Characters in dramas rarely present 'balanced' or 'reasonable' views. Here we notice that the Chorus illustrates its generalisations by reference to Samson's misfortunes with Dalila and the women of Timna; and that what the Danites are doing is attempting to solace Samson by complimenting him: if, in general, 'vertue, wisdom, valour, wit, / Strength, comliness of shape, or amplest merit' cannot 'win or long inherit' the love of women, Samson (they imply) ought not to take it as too personal an insult that his wives betrayed him: it is a common enough masculine misfortune. The reference to God's placing of the female in subjection to the male (1053–60) comes naturally after a recitation of the evils that come to men through women; considered in terms of Samson's own life it reminds us that his misfortunes are due not so much to lack of human prudence in dealing with his wives, but to his breaking of God's law in allowing himself to be swayed by his natural inferiors. He has thereby drawn confusion on his whole life. The Chorus is not merely twisting the knife in Samson's wound; for he has just demonstrated that he is not going to commit that error again.

HARAPHA
(1061–1267)

If we think of the action of *Samson* as taking place principally within the mind of the hero, we may feel by now that the 'turn' of the drama has occurred. Samson's encounter with Dalila, unlike that with his father, has wrung from him no expression of mental torture or despair. We do not even feel that his expressions of rage are particularly important in the development of the scene. In his encounter with Harapha, Samson makes explicit in the most positive manner what the audience has recently understood in the tone, and from what has *not* been said rather than what is said.

So far, Milton's demonstration of Samson's recovery of

Harapha

integrity has consisted of showing Samson's resistance to wrong action: we have witnessed great inner torment, accompanied by a 'wise passiveness' (to adapt Wordsworth's phrase). Now he is ready for action, though it does not yet appear what right action will be possible. The scene with Harapha is perfectly designed to make this clear: Harapha provokes Samson to an unmistakably truthful declaration of his readiness for action, while by his cowardice he makes the particular action proposed both unnecessary and impossible. The episode is only 'inconclusive' at the level of external event; for we now learn that Samson is ready to be 'God's champion' once more.

The question of Harapha's motivation is not important. It is raised, and quickly dismissed, by the Chorus at his entrance:

> Comes he in peace? what wind hath blown him hither
> I less conjecture than when first I saw
> The sumptuous Dalila floating this way:
> His habit carries peace, his brow defiance. (1070 ff.)

If we think of any roving bully on a Bank Holiday, we shall not be far wrong.

Samson's response, 'Or peace or not, alike to me he comes', expresses the strength of a mind which has been through despair and come out on the other side, not the indifference of torpor. This is made clear by the subsequent dialogue and nowhere more clear than in the masculine compression of his reply to Harapha's first speech: 'The way to know were not to see, but taste' (1091). Some two-thirds of the way through the drama, Samson offers to act.

I have already argued that we have been prepared for this moment, yet Milton ensures, by the startling brevity of Samson's reply to Harapha, that we are none the less surprised when it occurs. It foreshadows the moment when Samson decides to go to the Philistine games, in being a 'leap' or apparent discontinuity in the action, which has yet been dramatically prepared.

Samson's immediate response to Harapha, then, is to issue a direct challenge to single combat. There is no suggestion at this stage that Samson represents anything beyond himself, any principle beyond a justified irritation at impertinent chatter: 'Boast not of what thou wouldst have done, but do / What then thou wouldst, thou seest it in thy hand' (1104). Samson then moves to a more formal challenge, calling into question the tradition of chivalry represented by Harapha:

> put on all thy gorgeous arms, thy Helmet
> And Brigandine of brass, thy broad Habergeon,
> Vent-brass and Greves, and Gauntlet, add thy Spear
> A Weavers beam, and seven-times-folded shield,
> I onely with an Oak'n staff will meet thee.   (1119 ff.)

Then, in response to Harapha's accusation that Samson must be using 'spells / And black enchantments', Samson rediscovers his role as God's champion:

> I know no Spells, use no forbidd'n Arts;
> My trust is in the living God who gave me
> At my Nativity this strength, diffus'd
> No less through all my sinews, joints and bones,
> Then thine, while I preserv'd these locks unshorn,
> The pledge of my unviolated vow.
> For proof hereof, if *Dagon* be thy god,
> Go to his Temple, invocate his aid
> With solemnest devotion, spread before him
> How highly it concerns his glory now
> To frustrate and dissolve these Magic spells,
> Which I to be the power of *Israels* God
> Avow, and challenge *Dagon* to the test,
> Offering to combat thee his Champion bold,
> With th'utmost of his Godhead seconded:

Harapha

Then thou shalt see, or rather to thy sorrow
Soon feel, whose God is strongest, thine or mine.

(1139 ff.)

We notice that whereas earlier (59) Samson had spoken of his strength being hung in his hair, he now speaks of it as 'diffus'd ... through all my sinews, joints and bones'. His hair is merely a pledge of his 'unviolated vow' (rather like the fruit of the forbidden tree in *Paradise Lost*, which was 'indifferent' except as a pledge of the obedience of Adam and Eve). This speech, and the one following (1168 ff.), in which Samson expresses his faith in God's 'final pardon' should be sufficient to answer the objection (to Samson's defiance of Harapha) of one critic, who says: 'How this harmonises with the humility and contrition that are in order at this late stage of the regenerative process is a question worth raising.' There is nothing incompatible with humility or contrition in Samson's dealings with Harapha; there is nothing in him now of the former Samson who walked about 'like a petty God ... swoll'n with pride' (529). He no longer regards his strength as a personal possession, is no longer in danger of forgetting that it was given him by 'the living God' (1140). He is not provoking a brawl; he is offering himself as God's champion.

Samson was not written for the stage, but of course it has been acted. One imagines that a producer might find the characterisation of Harapha a problem. Is he a coward from the very beginning, or is he a brave man who crumbles before our eyes in the face of Samson's divinely inspired confidence? If the latter, then his disintegration is 'a miracle which is established by happening in our presence', as one critic says (arguing that Samson's regeneration is established for us by the remarkable collapse of Harapha). I think that the underlying assumption here is that we cannot believe quite so firmly in Samson's courage or his trust in God if Harapha is obviously a man of straw. But if we dig under *that* assumption do we not find the further assumption that at some time or other Samson's betrayal of God's cause and subsequent degradation had involved a failure in physical courage? And surely we have no reason to believe that that was ever the case.

Samson's physical courage has never been in doubt. What was in question, before the encounter with Harapha, was Samson's emergence from inner torment out into the possibility of positive action; what was in question was whether he would recover faith in his continued usefulness to God. So that what is important is not what Harapha represents in himself, but rather *the response he elicits from Samson*. In one sense it is true that the important thing in *Samson* is the hero's relationship with God rather than his relationship with other people. Yet Samson discovers – or re-discovers – his relationship with God through his encounters with other human beings. In that sense, one might borrow a famous phrase from Arnold Toynbee's *Study of History* and call *Samson* a drama of 'challenge and response'. I can perhaps best indicate my meaning by saying that what possibly remains a genuine problem for a producer does not seem to me a genuine problem for literary criticism. What matters is not so much whether Harapha is 'really' a coward or not, but the fact that the boasts he utters and the comments he passes are such as to assist Samson in the process of recovery.

In the Harapha episode Milton (characteristically) employs the resources of literary tradition, but transmutes them in accordance with his own purpose. One of his problems in writing this episode must have been that of keeping Harapha talking rather than fighting (or prematurely retreating). For the blusterer posing as a man of action there was a great deal of literary precedent, in classical times and in the Renaissance. The more recent precedents must have appealed considerably

Harapha

to Milton, since it had become the fashion to satirise the tradition of chivalry, the values of which Milton distrusted. The chivalric code of honour prescribed the conditions under which fighting should or should not be undertaken: for example a nobleman should not demean himself by fighting with one much below his station. While in general a gentleman or nobleman had to be prepared to defend his honour by fighting, many circumstances might arise in which it would be actually demeaning for him to fight. Sixteenth-century dramatists exploited this situation: a common character of farce is the braggart who invokes the restrictions of the chivalric code in order to escape fighting without confessing himself afraid. For example, the braggart would pretend to a noble status so that he could refuse to fight on the grounds that his opponent was base-born. (One of the more accessible examples for the student to to refer is Bobadill in Ben Jonson's *Every Man in his Humour*.)

Here, we see that Harapha boasts of being 'of stock renowned', says that he wishes he could have been present 'in camp or listed field' when Samson had performed his incredible feats, that is, when the code of honour would have permitted him (as it now forbids him) to oppose himself to Samson. When Samson says, in effect, 'There is no time like the present', Harapha again invokes the code of honour, which forbids him to fight with a blind man (see 1093 ff.; 1106). When Samson again challenges him, Harapha accuses him of employing 'spells / And black enchantments'. (Before duels, the combatants were supposed to swear that they did not rely on spells and enchantments: see the notes to this episode in G. and M. Bullough (eds), *Milton's Dramatic Poems*.)

If one reads this episode carefully, it will be seen that all of Harapha's excuses are variations on a single theme: the code of honour *forbids* him to combat with Samson. The order in which Milton introduces these various excuses enables him to achieve the progression I have remarked on: Samson progresses from a purely personal challenge to the moment when, in response to Harapha's accusation of sorcery, he offers himself as God's champion.

In view of the resemblance between Harapha and the farcical braggarts of many Renaissance comedies, the question has been raised of whether Milton does not fall into the error he condemns in his remarks prefatory to *Samson*, 'of intermixing Comic stuff with Tragic sadness and gravity'. One critic argues that (1) Milton here employs comic materials, (2) the result is not comic, (3) therefore Milton could not be funny even when he tried.

It seems to me, however, that Milton's originality here consists of using devices from comedy in order to solve a particular problem (providing a challenge for Samson to respond to while ensuring that Samson does not act yet) without allowing the predominant tone of his tragedy to be disturbed. In face of Samson, Harapha is indeed ridiculous, and Milton no doubt intended that he should be so; but the episode was not written *primarily* to satirise a warlike code of honour. Our principal attention throughout is focused on Samson, and there is no question of Milton having tried, and failed, to write a farcical episode. The means he employs to prevent Harapha from 'stealing the scene' may be safely left to the reader's own analysis.

SAMSON AND THE CHORUS
(1268–96)

The chief temptation besetting Samson is the temptation to despair, a despair which would have been confirmed, not relieved, if he had accepted the kind of life offered by Manoah or

Samson and the Chorus

by Dalila. Perhaps only those who have experienced it, or come very close to it, can fully realise how *seductive* despair can seem to the mind hard-pressed, how accurate it is to describe it as a temptation. (Again I refer the reader to Spenser's treatment of despair-as-seduction in *The Faerie Queene* I ix, especially stanzas 39-40.)

Harapha had obviously wished to tempt Samson to despair when he taunted:

> Presume not on thy God, what e're he be,
> Thee he regards not, owns not, hath cut off
> Quite from his people. (1156 ff.)

If these are insults they are insults which, in his earlier state of mind, Samson had offered to himself; but of course despair implies also an insult to God, an ultimate distrust in His mercy; and Samson will not tolerate such an insult to his God from a Philistine. To the challenge of Harapha's words Samson responds precisely with an affirmation that he does not despair (1168-76).

One of the signs by which we may apprehend Samson's new state of mind is the practical grasp he demonstrates in his discussion with the Danites, who fear (1250-52) that Samson's defiance of Harapha will cause further trouble. In his reply (1253-67) Samson points out cogently enough why it is unlikely that Harapha will feel able to 'stir up' the Lords to afflict him further. It is a small point, and it is perhaps inflating it to remind the reader of the enhanced practical ability which students of mysticism see as the mystic's reward for surviving the 'dark night of the soul'. At least the reader will agree that Samson shows good practical judgement here, and that this is not insignificant. If we have been asking ourselves, 'If God revealed His will to Samson now, could he act on the revelation?' we could, at this point, give a positive answer.

The Danites' next speech ('O how comely it is and how reviving' (1268 ff.)) is a natural response to Samson's newly recovered vigour of mood. I have anticipated this speech in writing earlier of patience (see the commentary on 652 ff.) and can here deal with it very briefly.

The Chorus's speech deals with the two kinds of fortitude (magnanimity and patience) from lines 1268–96. One may well see in the tone of the earlier part a natural elation at the possibility that Samson may yet be capable of heroic action, and in the tone of what follows a sober acceptance of the likelihood that he may have to be content with heroic suffering. There is an irony, of course, which will not be apparent to the Danites until after Samson's death: that is, Samson is able to 'have it both ways'; his pulling down of the temple upon himself and the Philistines unites both kinds of fortitude; it is an action which is also a suffering.

SAMSON AND THE OFFICER
(1297–1426)

The 'action' of this section is outwardly simple. The Officer demands Samson's presence at Dagon's feast. Samson refuses. The Officer goes to convey this refusal to the Philistine lords, and very shortly returns and repeats the demand. This time Samson agrees, and goes off with the Officer.

We may ask why Samson at first refuses, and then accedes to the Officer's demand. Samson (addressing himself to the Chorus) tells us. He refuses the first time because as a Nazarite, dedicated to purity of life, he will not add to the sins he has already committed 'by prostituting holy things to Idols'. (We notice here, as in the dialogue after Harapha's exit, that Samson is no longer immersed in consideration of his past. He is living in the present, and again, in reply to the Chorus's

'Where the heart joins not, outward acts defile not' (1368) Samson demonstrates a practical grasp of the situation: 'Commands are no constraints.') His decision to go with the Officer should not be seen simply as a 'change of mind', or even (as one critic would have it) as marking a total break with his earlier refusal. Surely, what this episode is largely about is the relationship between the 'forms' and the inner meaning of religious experience. By his earlier sins Samson, especially dedicated to God, had defiled himself. Lines 606–32 expressed his sense of that defilement, in terms of diseases which do not stop at the body's surface but 'Ranckle, and fester, and gangrene, / To black mortification' (621). The whole passage expresses the sort of corruption which water can never cleanse, but which can only be dealt with by the terrible action of fire. (The reader should consider the relevance of the 'holocaust' (1700 ff.) and its relation to the repeated description of the 'flames' which heralded Samson's birth (22–9; 1431–35).

In the action of the drama so far, we have seen, however agonisingly slow it has been, a process of regeneration. If that were not the case, there would surely be something so unrealistic as to be pathetic in Samson's present insistence on ritual purity. It is not pathetic, because Samson has won the right so to insist. The ritual purity on which he insists is the emblem of his regained ability to act as 'God's servant'. But, once regained, that ability may lead him to do again what, as God's servant, he has done before; that is, to overturn religious custom. Ritual purity for Samson at this moment is an emblem of inner purity; now he may go on to transcend it.

If we think back upon Samson's career, we notice that inspiration has before now come to him as permission to overturn religious custom. Earlier, he had married the woman of Timna (220), his personal relationship with God sanctioning an action which would ordinarily have been defiling. The point is, that there is no outward sign of religious observance which God may not on occasion dispense with. The hard thing, as Samson demonstrated when he married Dalila, is to distinguish our secret desires from the quiet promptings of God within our minds. The real sign of the genuineness of Samson's spiritual recovery (which he, quite rightly, celebrates by his refusal to defile himself at Dagon's feast) is that when the prompting of God occurs again he recognises it for what it is! He could, after all, have so easily dismissed it as a rationalisation of cowardice.

CHORUS
(1427–40)

Samson goes with the Officer, followed by the blessing of his countrymen. We have seen Samson recall again and again his past failures; we have seen him slowly moving towards the moment when he is able to deal firmly with challenges of the present as posed by Harapha and the Officer; we have seen him suddenly moving on again, so that he can now, however obscurely, envisage a meaningful future for himself: 'I with this Messenger will go along' (1384).

Samson's rediscovered confidence in his own destiny has communicated itself to the Danites, who pray, not for his protection, but for his usefulness as God's servant:

> Go, and the Holy One
> Of *Israel* be thy guide
> To what may serve his glory best, and spread his name
> Great among the Heathen round:
> Send thee the Angel of thy Birth, to stand
> Fast by thy side, who from thy Fathers field

Rode up in flames after his message told
Of thy conception, and be now a shield
Of fire. (1427-35)

We remember that the prophecy of Samson's birth has been recalled before (22 ff.). There, it was put forward as an incomprehensible, apparently meaningless past history. Here, the Chorus recalls the angel's fiery ascent in a passage that looks to the future, their words ringing with confidence that Samson's earlier 'wherefore?' would find its answer. It does, of course, and is interpreted for us in the image of the phoenix which occurs near the close of the play (1699 ff.).

MANOAH, CHORUS, AND MESSENGER (1441-1659)

Now that Samson has left the stage we are reminded that Manoah, even though his name signifies 'rest', has not been idle. Previously, we have seen him in the guise of unconscious tempter. Now, we learn that he is more like Samson than we had realised: he has his own brand of heroism. There is of course an ironic gap between Manoah's hopes for Samson and the events that are taking place off-stage as he relates those hopes to the Chorus; but it would be unjust to regard Manoah's hopes, mistaken as they are, as ignoble. There is a partial truth perhaps in the judgement of one critic that: 'Manoa still lives in the past... [he] still conceives of Samson (as Dalila did) as a passive object set up for the emotions of others.' After all, Manoah has not, as we have, witnessed Samson's encounters with Dalila, Harapha, and the Officer; the gap between the hero and those around him is of the essence of tragedy. Nevertheless, in his account of the importuning of the Philistine lords (1457-71), we see Manoah's willingness to undergo humiliation: the account humbly mirrors Samson's willingness to play the fool at Dagon's games while he awaits God's final revelation. Moreover, we see now that Manoah's hopes for his son's future reach out beyond the idea of Samson's ease, to include 'purpose', 'use', and 'service' (1498–9).

Manoah's scheming on Samson's behalf provides the nearest thing to a 'sub-plot' the drama can show. By putting Manoah centrally on stage at this point Milton provides both an ironic counterpointing of the catastrophe and a relaxation of tension (after the remarkable development of Samson's confrontation with the Officer) upon which the great final scene impinges with great effect. Even a Johnsonian reader, one imagines, would concede that, whether or not hastened or retarded by the intermediate parts, the catastrophe is superbly managed.

Milton has frequently been accused of lacking visual imagination, but I am inclined to believe that he could, if he had lived in our time, have made a contribution to the cinema. Once again we see him employ the technique of bringing his subject gradually into sharper focus, from the moment of the 'hideous noise' which provokes Manoah's exclamation (1509) to the graphic description by the Messenger (1596–1659). This is the scene for which the entire drama hitherto has been preparing us; it combines the immediacy of visual presentation with the intimate shaping of response and understanding which only language can achieve.

One may sense the care with which Milton has constructed the final episode by noting how unnatural the long speech of the Messenger might have seemed, how trivial and self-regarding its beginnings, if he had not been invited by Manoah to proceed in this way:

> Tell us the sum, the circumstance deferr. (1557)

> More than anough we know; but while things yet
> Are in confusion, give us if thou canst,

> Eye-witness of what first or last was done,
> Relation more particular and distinct. (1592–5)

This gives the Messenger occasion to develop his story at length, in his own way, from his own point of view. It is both humanly natural, and faithful to the facts from his standpoint, that the Messenger begins by telling it as *his* story, down to 'I among these aloof obscurely stood'. It is, when we think of it, a natural progression: initial consciousness of the separate self, the merging of the self with the crowd, the concentration on a great event so absolute that one's private significance is caught up in the action witnessed. The movement of the Messenger's account beautifully exemplifies the way in which the individual ego is transcended in face of the high tragic event.

The event narrated is such that stage representation is intrinsically impossible; but the quality of the writing ensures that nothing is thereby lost. The reader is caught up into the audience, becomes one of those among whom the Messenger 'obscurely stood'. We see, not merely the external ruin, but the precedent moment of stillness which links this final, external action with the intense inward action which has filled the drama so far:

> ... with head a while enclin'd,
> And eyes fast fixt he stood, as one who pray'd,
> Or some great matter in his mind revolv'd. (1636 ff.)

We may link this with the Chorus's earlier perception of Samson's double armoury, of 'celestial vigour' (implying supernatural aid) and 'plain heroic magnitude of mind'. The two passages taken together show how false to Milton's drama is the dilemma posed by some critics, and posed by Milton himself in his *Defence of the English People*, when he recognised the alternatives of whether Samson 'acted in pursuance of a command from heaven or was prompted by his own valour'. Surely they answer the criticism that the harmony of God's will and Samson's comes 'not from any interaction between them, but from God's will being exerted and overruling Samson's'. A. S. P. Woodhouse is surely correct in saying that in *Samson* Milton does not choose between the two views which are opposed in the *Defence*, but rather combines and harmonises them, as is indicated at this crucial moment, when Samson both prays and thinks: 'he was in fact doing both. Granted that the outcome is controlled by God's overruling power, and that his grace is operative from the first, though overtly so only as the catastrophe approaches, yet Samson's responses are at every point natural and humanly intelligible. If he is an instrument of Providence, he does not cease to be an individual, fallible, though corrigible, heroic ... and by his own action doomed.' ('Tragic Effect in *Samson Agonistes*,' *University of Toronto Quarterly*, xxviii (1959), 205–22.) It is perhaps relevant to notice here the final image of Samson as Phoenix: 'that self-begott'n bird' (1699).

After the Chorus's necessary justification for Samson's suicide ('not willingly, but tangl'd in the fold / Of dire necessity') Milton splits the Chorus into two halves (1669–1707). The first Semichorus (1659–86) expresses a clear, natural – one might say 'primitive' or 'Old Testament' – commentary on the catastrophe. The second (1687–1707), more complex, brings perhaps nearer to the surface than hitherto the traditional interpretation of Samson as a prototype of Christ, certainly brings together some important thematic strands, and requires close attention.

At the end of the first Semichorus, Samson's blindness has been transferred, in a metaphorical sense, to the Philistines. Samson, by contrast, is now 'With inward eyes illuminated'. We may remember Manoah's hope, expressed not so long ago:

Manoah, Chorus, and Messenger

And since his strength with eye-sight was not lost,
God will restore him eye-sight to his strength.   (1502)

The Greek meaning of 'dragon' is 'seeing one'. The noun is derived from a verb meaning 'to have a particular look in one's eyes', and referring not so much to the function of the eye as to its gleam as noticed by someone else. Milton's image is that of domestic fowls transfixed by a serpent: by the look in his eyes Samson mesmerises the Philistines. By its very meaning, the word 'dragon' opposes the spiritual sight of Samson to the spiritual blindness of the Philistines. It is by the attainment of spiritual vision that Samson gains power, symbolised by the Eagle, and the capacity for spiritual rebirth, symbolised by the Phoenix.

It is important to notice that each term in this developing metaphor involves a *winged* creature: dragon, fowls, eagle, phoenix. In *Of Reformation in England* Milton refers to the winged dragon of heraldry, and we should notice here that the word 'Assailant' is a heraldic term: a dragon 'salient' would have its hind feet on the ground, and its forefeet up – as here 'on the perched roosts / And nests in order rang'd' (1693).

Throughout the poem so far, our image of Samson has been that of a blind, motionless, enslaved man. The complex image of the ending expresses vision, movement, freedom. The freedom and the rebirth of the Phoenix arise from entombment and apparent extinction, just as the regained freedom of Samson arises from imposed imprisonment and voluntary extinction of self. The image both looks back over the action of the drama and establishes Samson as a prototype of Christ: the Phoenix arising from its own ashes is of course an emblem of the Resurrection. It also links up with the earlier image of the prophetic angel ascending in flames, and answers the question Samson had asked in despair at the drama's opening:

> O wherefore was my birth from Heav'n foretold
> Twice by an Angel, who at last in sight
> Of both my Parents all in flames ascended
> From off the Altar, where an Off'ring burnd,
> As in a fiery column charioting
> His Godlike presence, and from some great act
> Or benefit reveald to *Abraham's* race? (23 ff.)

The closing lines of *Samson* (1755 ff.) beautifully formulate Aristotle's doctrine of catharsis (or mental purgation) arising from the tragic experience. Yet the drama itself does not perfectly accord with the description of tragedy which Aristotle derived from his experience of Greek drama. (No predominantly good man is brought to an evil end through some fatal flaw, for example.) Though the structure of Samson points us to Greek tragedy, the question of whether it *is* a tragedy would probably have to be answered negatively if Greek tragedy were our sole criterion. A. S. P. Woodhouse has performed a service in pointing out that, different as *Samson* may appear to be in structure and spirit from Shakespeare's tragedies, a theory of tragedy based upon Shakespeare's work would probably account for the sources of tragic emotion in *Samson* more adequately than would a reading of the *Poetics* or of Greek tragedy.

If Samson's fate does not follow the guidelines of Aristotle, it still evokes emotions of terror and pity, the more profoundly for the intimacy with which we have come to know him. And while it is true that the hero's relationship with God, rather than his relationship with his fellow-men, is the important thing, nevertheless Samson is felt to be representative of his society, to embody its sins, its courage and its hope of ultimate redemption. As in Shakespeare, so here: an important element in the tragic experience is our sense of a moral order re-established after a period of subversion. That is the significance of Manoah's final speech, setting Samson's death in a national context in which the reader participates, and expressing a sense of regained peace and order:

> To *Israel*
> Honour hath left, and freedom, let but them
> Find courage to lay hold on this occasion,
> To himself and Fathers house eternal fame.
>
> (1714 ff.)

The moral order has been restored. The hero's task has been accomplished. Samson is dead, but his heroism is felt to be more impressive than his end is terrifying. The life of his community will go on, and will be the better for his sacrifice and example. It is the significance for Samson's society that Manoah finally invokes, as he celebrates the 'peace and consolation', the 'true experience from this great event', by looking into the future:

> Thither shall all the valiant youth resort,
> And from his memory inflame thir brests
> To matchless valour, and adventures high.
>
> (1738 ff.)

Questions for Discussion

1. Write on Milton's adaptation of the Biblical story of Samson.
2. Write on 'the theme of heroism' in *Samson Agonistes*. (If you know Milton's other major poems, attempt a comparative study.)
3. What elements in *Samson Agonistes* do you consider to be (*a*) Hebraic, (*b*) Greek, (*c*) Christian?
4. Write on the role of the Chorus in *Samson Agonistes*.
5. Compare the diction and versification of *Samson Agonistes* with that of *Comus*.
6. Discuss the view that *Samson Agonistes* is primarily about God's 'providence' and only incidentally about the 'regeneration' of Samson.
7. '*Samson Agonistes* read aloud would be hardly tolerable, because of [the] loss in the poet of all feeling for his native English.' (F. R. Leavis.) Discuss.

Further Reading

Reference

The Bible

Cruden's Concordance (Lutterworth, rev. ed., 1954).

The Oxford Classical Dictionary (Oxford, Clarendon Press, 1949).

J. H. Hanford, *A Milton Handbook* (Appleton-Century-Crofts, New York, 4th ed., 1946).

The Oxford English Dictionary should be consulted whenever it is suspected that Milton is using a word in a sense now obsolete.

The Shorter Oxford English Dictionary is also useful.

Editions

Milton's Dramatic Poems, ed. Geoffrey and Margaret Bullough (Athlone Press, 1958).

The Student's Milton, ed. F. A. Patterson (Appleton-Century-Crofts, New York, 2nd ed., 1933). The complete poems and all the important prose works.

The Poetical Works of John Milton, ed. Helen Darbishire (Oxford, Clarendon Press, vol. ii, 1955).

Samson Agonistes, ed. F. T. Prince (Cambridge University Press, 1951).

Criticism

F. M. Krouse, *Milton's Samson and the Christian Tradition* (Princeton University Press, 1949).

W. R. Parker, *Milton's Debt to Greek Tragedy in Samson Agonistes* (Johns Hopkins Press, 1937).

Arnold Stein, *Heroic Knowledge: An Interpretation of Paradise Regained and Samson Agonistes* (University of Minnesota Press, 1957).

J. B. Broadbent, *Milton: Comus and Samson Agonistes* (Edward Arnold, 1961).

F. T. Prince, 'The Choruses of Samson Agonistes', in *The Italian Element in Milton's Verse* (Oxford, Clarendon Press, 1954; corrected ed., 1962).